Being Your Best at Cheerleading

NEL YOMTOV

Children's Press®
An Imprint of Scholastic Inc.

Content Consultant
Barry Wilner
Associated Press
New York City, New York

Library of Congress Cataloging-in-Publication Data
Names: Yomtov, Nelson.
Title: Being your best at cheerleading / by Nel Yomtov.
Description: New York : Children's Press An Imprint of Scholastic Inc., 2016.
   | 2017. | Series: A True Book | Includes bibliographical references,
   webography and index.
Identifiers: LCCN 2015048714| ISBN 9780531232651 (library binding) | ISBN
   9780531236161 (paperback)
Subjects: LCSH: Cheerleading—Juvenile literature.
Classification: LCC LB3635 .Y57 2016 | DDC 791.6/4—dc23
LC record available at http://lccn.loc.gov/2015048714

Front cover: Cheerleaders
performing a scorpion stunt

Back cover: A cheerleader
jumping with pom-poms

Find the Truth!

Everything you are about to read is true *except* for one of the sentences on this page.

Which one is **TRUE**?

T or F The fist and the blade are names of cheerleading hand motions.

T or F A flyer is the person in a stunt who supports or tosses another cheerleader.

Find the answers in this book.

3

Contents

THE **BIG** TRUTH!

A partner stunt

A cheerleading squad jumps together.

A lunge

Several U.S. presidents were [ ] cheerleaders, including George W. Bush and Franklin Delano Roosevelt.

Skilled cheerleaders [ ]n wow crowds with their amazing abilities.

CHAPTER 1

Getting Started

Cheerleading combines graceful, powerful movements and team spirit. Like any sport, cheerleading involves training, practice, and competitiveness. Teamwork is also essential. Cheerleaders must work as a group to perform difficult routines and **stunts**. From inspiring the crowd at a game to wowing the judges at a competition, this sport can be both challenging and rewarding. And with hard work and practice, you can become your best at cheerleading.

Some cheerleaders are good at difficult acrobatic moves.

More Than Cheers

A **squad** member's voice is an important part of leading a cheer, but it's not everything. Many routines involve jumping, tumbling, and dancing. Cheerleaders often hold up or toss their teammates into the air. This requires agility and balance. Each cheerleader in a squad has his or her own particular talents and abilities. There's a range of parts to play in this high-energy sport.

Sidelines and Center Stage

There are two main types of cheerleading: sideline and competition. Sideline cheering pumps up the fans' spirits at a sporting event, inspiring them to cheer for their team. Cheer routines are performed during time-outs and halftimes, as well as during the action of the game.

Competition cheerleading is a sport that pits squad against squad. Squads perform routines for judges, who award points for technique, creativity, and coordination. The team with the highest score wins.

Equipment

Cheerleading does not require a lot of fancy, expensive equipment. Here's a checklist of the essentials.

 Uniforms: Girls usually wear skirts or shorts, and matching tops. Boys wear loose tops and matching shorts or gym pants.

 Shoes: Well-fitting, rubber-soled sneakers that support the ankles are ideal.

 Megaphones: These cone-shaped devices are often used to **amplify** the voice and lead crowds in cheers.

Megaphones first became widely used in the 1900s.

Pom-poms: These attract attention to the cheerleaders. They are usually made of paper or plastic strips, or sometimes of wool, cotton, or even feathers.

 Signs: Signs encourage the crowd and get them excited about the event.

 Tumbling mats: If you're going to perform any tumbling or acrobatic stunts, use a tumbling mat. It will help cushion you in case you fall.

Pom-poms

Uniform top

Uniform skirt

Pom-poms often match the colors of a cheerleader's uniform.

Sneakers

Stretching improves the body's flexibility and agility and can help you avoid injury.

Training and Warm-Up Tips

You need strength, agility, and endurance as a cheerleader. These tools can improve the quality of your stunts and routines. They also help reduce your risk of injury while performing demanding acrobatics. Taking care of your body starts with stretching your muscles before cheering. Stretch your whole body: the upper and lower legs, hips, back, arms, and neck. This will make you tuned up and ready for action.

It is important to maintain good form as you do push-ups.

Strength

Building strength will increase the power in your muscles. You can visit a gym and lift weights, but you don't have to. You can also train in the comfort and privacy of your home. Try push-ups to work on your arms and chest. Sit-ups will strengthen your abs and lower back muscles. To work your upper leg muscles, do squats and leg lunges. Toe-raises are great to develop your calf muscles.

Endurance

Endurance is the ability of the body's muscles to work over a long period of time. It is essential for most sports, including cheerleading. Almost any physical activity that increases your heart rate will help improve your endurance. Walking, jogging, bike riding, basketball, and soccer are great examples. Roller-skating, ice-skating, and dancing also do wonders for your endurance.

Whenever you train, pay attention to your body. If you feel faint or dizzy, stop and rest.

Jogging is a great way to build endurance and stay in shape.

Strengthening Your Voice

Whether shouting to a crowd or communicating with your teammates, your voice is an important part of cheerleading. Just as your muscles and limbs require stretching, your voice needs to warm up as well. Try humming. You can also buzz the tongue by making a "zzzzzz" sound. Trill your lips with a "brrrrr" sound, and roll the tongue by making a "trrrrr" sound. Use these exercises to "warm down" after cheering, too.

Chanting and yelling play a big role in cheerleading.

A Deep Breath

Yoga classes are a great way to improve your breathing.

When cheering, breathe deeply from your diaphragm, the muscle just under your lungs. Exercise your diaphragm for 5 to 10 minutes a few times each day:

1. Lie on your back on a flat surface. Keep your knees bent. Support your head with a pillow or towel. Place one hand on your chest and the other on your stomach.

2. Breathe in through your nose so your stomach moves out against your hand.

3. Breathe out through your lips, tightening your stomach. Feel your stomach fall inward.

4. Throughout the exercise, try to limit how much your chest expands up against your hand.

Keeping a smile on your face as you perform can be trickier than it sounds.

CHAPTER 3

Basic Cheerleading Motions

Whether cheering in front of a crowd or a panel of judges, try to look like you're having fun! Facial expressions, or "facials," can fire up an audience. Smile even when you're performing difficult stunts. Give a brisk shake of the head or a wink. Facials should be exaggerated, or larger than life, and match your movements and chants. You can practice in front of a mirror to make your expressions picture-perfect.

Pom-poms were invented in the 1930s.

A group of cheerleaders shows off a clasp position.

Basic Hand Positions

There are four basic cheerleading hand positions.

 Fist: Make a fist with your thumb on the outside. Keep your wrists straight.

Blade: With your arm straight out, extend your fingers and keep them tightly together.

Clasp: Bring your hands together in front of your chest. Wrap your thumbs and fingers tightly around each other.

Clap: Place your palms together so they are flat and touching in front of your chest.

Arm Motions

Your arms help communicate motion and emotion to the audience. To do the high-V motion, point your arms up in a V shape tilted slightly forward. In a low-V, the arms are in a downward V shape. In a T motion, both arms are held straight out to the side. For a punch up, thrust one arm straight up and place the other hand on your hip. Always perform your arm motions with straight wrists.

Arm motions are often done with fists, though squads might use other hand signs.

Lunges

A cheerleading lunge can be done toward the front or the side. In both cases, one leg stays straight with the toes pointing forward. The other leg bends. Follow these helpful tips.

1. *Forward lunge:* Keep your back leg straight. Step the other leg forward and bend that knee toward the audience.

2. *Side lunge:* Step out a little wider than hip distance. Bend one leg, pointing that foot to the side. You can lunge to the left or the right.

Use "spirit fingers" as you cheer. Quickly wiggle your fingers with straight, outstretched arms.

Lunges require strength and flexibility.

High kicks are an advanced cheerleading technique.

Kicks

Exciting, high-energy leg kicks are an important part of many cheers. Kicks require great balance and flexibility. During the kick, keep one foot on the ground with the leg straight. Keep your kicking leg straight, too, and point your kicking toes. You can kick to the front, side, or back. Your back should be as straight as possible. Work on lower, simple kicks first. Only after you master those should you try high kicks.

Cheering Is for Boys

Women have dominated the sport of cheerleading for decades. But back in the 1800s, cheerleading got its start as a male-only activity. Today, male cheerleaders still play an important role on the sidelines. Besides getting the crowd fired up, they add a big boost to some of the more challenging performances.

Pyramids, which can be 2 1/2 people high (the top person held at waist height) or higher.

Men tend to have stronger upper bodies than women, especially when it comes to arms and shoulders. This strength helps provide a solid foundation for high-flying stunts. Just a few examples are:

Partner stunts such as a toss to hands or a full up stretch. Partner stunts are performed with a single base and a flyer.

Basket toss, in which two or more bases toss a flyer as high as 18 feet (5.5 meters) into the air. They catch her with joined arms.

High school rules
forbid spotters to
have their hands
behind their back
during a stunt.

Stunts and Jumps

Stunting is among the most exciting parts of cheerleading. Setting up complex formations or being tossed into the air can be fun. But it can also be dangerous. Always take extreme care. A basic stunt includes a **base** of at least one person and the **flyer**, or the top person. Every stunt also includes a **spotter** to catch the flyer at the end of the stunt. Jumping, like stunting, requires concentration, split-second timing, and flexibility.

Stunting

One basic stunt is the elevator. It requires two bases, one spotter, and the flyer. The bases face each other, arms against their sides. The flyer stands between the bases, facing forward. The spotter stands behind the flyer with his or her hands on the flyer's waist. The flyer lifts one leg and steps into the palms of one of the bases. As this base lifts, the other base places his or her palms under the flyer's opposite foot.

Bases must be strong enough to make sure their teammates do not fall during stunts.

Both bases lift the flyer, bringing their hands to rest at their chest level. To **dismount**, the bases lower the flyer back onto the ground.

A more advanced stunt is called the scorpion. The flyer stands on one leg while being lifted high in the air. She bends her other leg back and, reaching over her head and back, grabs the toes with both hands. You need excellent balance and flexibility for this pose.

A scorpion is difficult to pull off, but very impressive to audiences.

It takes a lot of practice to do a successful spread eagle.

Jumping

The front hurdler, toe touch, pike, tuck, and spread eagle are among the most common cheer jumps.

Jumps have four steps: the approach, the lift, the jump, and the landing, together performed in eight counts.

🎀 *Approach (counts 1 and 2):* Stand with your legs together. Start with your hands at your side, then move them into a clasp.

🎀 *Lift (3 and 4):* Throw your arms into a high-V and rise up on your toes.

Jump (5 and 6): Swing your arms down past your sides. Bend your knees as you go into a slight crouch. You're now prepared for takeoff! Spring up off your toes into the jump.

 Landing (7 and 8): Land on the balls of your feet, legs together and knees bent to absorb the impact. To finish, stand up straight, with your shoulders back and head held high.

The cheerleaders on a team often perform the same jump all at once.

You will need to be at the top of your game to succeed at cheerleading tryouts.

Acing Your Tryout

For many cheerleading squads, you have to try out to join. Before you put in long hours of practice, find out what the squad expects of you. How often are practices, games, and competitions held? Will you have to attend camps or other events the squad or your school conducts? If you have the desire, the time, and the right attitude, you're ready to practice!

 More than half of all cheerleaders play another sport.

Dance classes are a great way to improve flexibility and learn skills you can use in cheerleading.

Before Tryouts

Before tryout day, you often need to attend practices or clinics. These usually last a week. There, you learn the cheers and routines you'll perform at the tryouts. But don't wait for those practices to start preparing. Spend days or weeks stretching and exercising. Yoga or classes in dance, such as jazz, hip-hop, or ballet, can help you fine-tune your dancing skills. You can work on tumbling and acrobatics in gymnastics classes.

Week of Practices

When the official clinic begins, attend every practice. Stay positive and enthusiastic. Don't be shy: Ask questions if you don't understand something. After each practice, review the routines in your head and write down the words to the cheers. On the first day of practice, ask if you may have a copy of the music for the routines and dances. You can use it to practice the routines at home in front of a mirror.

Practicing is the only way to get good enough to pull off advanced cheerleading techniques.

35

The Big Day

Get plenty of sleep the night before the tryouts. Eat a healthy breakfast and lunch that day. Dress comfortably in clothes you can move around in easily. If possible, you can even wear your school colors. Your coach may tell you what you should wear. If not, ask about it at practice.

Timeline of Cheerleading History

1880s

Students at Princeton University lead a cheer at a football game. The practice of cheerleading begins to take off.

1923

The first female cheerleaders join the squad at the University of Minnesota.

1898

Jack Campbell organizes the first official cheerleading squad.

When it's your turn, take a deep breath and smile! Perform the routines with confidence, energy, and spirit. Make eye contact with the judges. Shout your cheer sharply and cleanly. Use your best facials and spirit fingers to impress the judges. If you mess up, just keep smiling and continue your cheers. When you finish, thank the judges and leave the area quietly.

1950s
The Baltimore Colts football team hires the first professional cheerleading squad.

1948
Lawrence Herkimer starts the world's first cheerleading clinic in Texas.

2004
Walt Disney World in Florida hosts the first World Cheerleading Championships.

Following Your Dream

If you make the squad, congratulations! If you did not, that's okay. There may be another squad to try out for, and there's always next year. You can also ask the coach if there's another way to be part of the team. Stay positive and continue to pursue your goal. No matter what happens, congratulate the people who made the squad. Politely accept the decision of the judges and thank them and your coach.

Always keep a positive attitude, even if things don't go the way you want them to.

Pyramids

Cheerleading pyramids combine various lifts, poses, and dismounts to create a spectacular stunt. Among the many types of pyramids are the simple pyramid and the inside hitch. Note how spotters are on the ground, prepared to catch the flyer if he or she falls.

Simple pyramid

Inside hitch

Spotter

Spotter

Spotter

Competing in front of judges can be stressful, but very rewarding.

CHAPTER 6

Competitors and Professionals

There are dozens of cheerleading organizations in the United States and around the world. These groups work to make cheerleading a fun, safe, and competitive sport. They establish rules and organize national and international competitions. Competitions include solo performances, teams, and stunt groups. On the local level, high school squads compete in **regional** and state competitions.

About 600 women try out for the Dallas Cowboys' cheerleading squad each year. Only 45 are selected for the practice squad.

Major Organizations

The National Cheerleaders Association (NCA), founded in 1948, is the oldest cheerleading organization. The NCA hosts high school and college national and high school regional championships in the United States. The International Federation of Cheerleading formed in 1998. It trains coaches and judges, and conducts world championships. The International Cheer Union hosts international and regional cheer and dance championships.

A squad competes in a National Cheerleaders Association event.

Professional NFL cheerleader Teneeka Miller teaches students basic cheerleading moves at a training camp.

Professional Cheering

Do you want to take your team spirit beyond your school days? Professional cheering might be for you. Most professional football and basketball teams employ cheerleaders and dancers. These squads perform before games, during time-outs, and at halftimes. They also often help raise money for charities, visit schools, and teach cheerleading skills to young people. They are great examples of people being their best at cheerleading. ★

True Statistics

Number of cheerleaders worldwide: 4.6 million in 79 countries

Number of cheerleaders in the United States: 3.3 million (2013)

Percent of cheerleaders involved in a second sport: About 62

Percent of U.S. schools with cheerleading squads: About 80

Percent of U.S. cheerleaders who are female: About 97

Percent of college cheerleaders who are male: 50

Number of National Football League (NFL) teams with a cheerleading squad: 26 of 32 teams

Average per-game salary of an NFL cheerleader: $70 to $150

Did you find the truth?

(T) The fist and the blade are names of cheerleading hand motions.

(F) A flyer is the person in a stunt who supports or tosses another cheerleader.

Resources

Books

Hunt, Sara R. *You've Got Spirit! Cheers, Chants, Tips, and Tricks Every Cheerleader Needs to Know*. Minneapolis: Millbrook Press, 2013.

Rissman, Rebecca. *Jump, Tuck, Flip: Mastering Cheerleading Skills and Stunts*. North Mankato, MN: Capstone Press, 2016.

Rissman, Rebecca. *Show Your Spirit: Cheerleading Basics You Need to Know*. North Mankato, MN: Capstone Press, 2016.

Visit this Scholastic Web site for more information on being your best at cheerleading:

★ www.factsfornow.scholastic.com

Enter the keywords **Being Your Best at Cheerleading**

Important Words

amplify (AM-pli-fye) to make something stronger

base (BAYSS) a cheerleader who lifts, holds, or tosses flyers into the air during a stunt

dismount (dis-MOUNT) to get off or down

flyer (FLYE-uhr) a cheerleader who is lifted, held, or tossed into the air during a stunt

regional (REE-juh-nuhl) relating to a general area or a specific district or territory

spotter (SPAHT-uhr) a cheerleader who lifts, supports, or catches another cheerleader during a stunt

squad (SKWAD) a small group of people who work or are involved in the same activity

stunts (STUHNTS) acrobatic moves that involve lifting, tossing, or holding another person

Index

Page numbers in **bold** indicate illustrations.

About the Author

Nel Yomtov is an award-winning author with a passion for writing nonfiction books for young readers. He has written books and graphic novels about history, geography, science, and other subjects.

Nel has worked at Marvel Comics, where he edited, wrote, and colored hundreds of titles. He has also served as editorial director of a children's book publisher and as publisher of Hammond World Atlas books.

Yomtov lives in the New York City area with his wife, Nancy, a teacher. Their son, Jess, is a sports journalist.